Reading 0118 9015950
Battle   0118 9015100
sham 0118 901510
        0118 901510
                015109
                    12

KT-168-697

Homework Helpers

the SAXONS and the VIKINGS

by *Alison Howard*
Consultant: Alice Proctor

READING BOROUGH COUNCIL	
3412600276043	
PETERS	05-Mar-2010
CH941.01	

Reading Borough Council

34126002760430

How to use this book

Each topic in this book is clearly labelled and contains all these components:

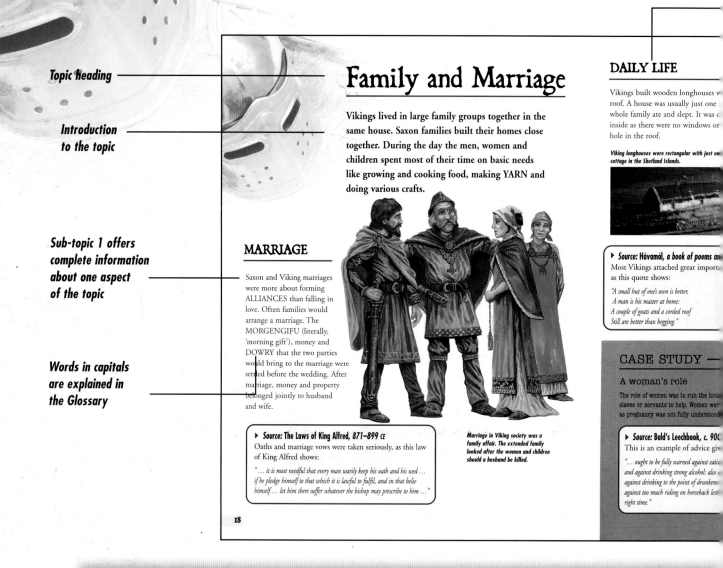

Topic heading

Introduction to the topic

Sub-topic 1 offers complete information about one aspect of the topic

Words in capitals are explained in the Glossary

Family and Marriage

Vikings lived in large family groups together in the same house. Saxon families built their homes close together. During the day the men, women and children spent most of their time on basic needs like growing and cooking food, making YARN and doing various crafts.

MARRIAGE

Saxon and Viking marriages were more about forming ALLIANCES than falling in love. Often families would arrange a marriage. The MORGENGIFU (literally, 'morning gift'), money and DOWRY that the two parties would bring to the marriage were settled before the wedding. After marriage, money and property belonged jointly to husband and wife.

▶ **Source: The Laws of King Alfred, 871–899 CE**
Oaths and marriage vows were taken seriously, as this law of King Alfred shows:

"… it is most needful that every man warily keep his oath and his wed … if he pledge himself to that which it is lawful to fulfil, and in that belie himself'… let him there suffer whatever the bishop may prescribe to him …"

Marriage in Viking society was a family affair. The extended family looked after the women and children should a husband be killed.

18

DAILY LIFE

Vikings built wooden longhouses w roof. A house was usually just one whole family ate and slept. It was c inside as there were no windows or hole in the roof.

Viking longhouses were rectangular with just on cottage in the Shetland Islands.

▶ **Source: Hávamál, a book of poems an**
Most Vikings attached great importa as this quote shows:

*"A small hut of one's own is better,
A man is his master at home:
A couple of goats and a corded roof
Still are better than begging."*

CASE STUDY —

A woman's role

The role of women was to run the hou slaves or servants to help. Women wer as pregnancy was not fully understood

▶ **Source: Bald's Leechbook, c. 90C**
This is an example of advice giv

"… ought to be fully warned against eati and against drinking strong alcohol: also against drinking to the point of drunkenn against too much riding on horseback lest right time."

ISBN 978 1 84898 077 8

This edition published in 2009 by *ticktock* Media Ltd

Printed in China

9 8 7 6 5 4 3 2 1

A CIP catalogue record for this book is available from the British Library.

All rights reserved. No part of this publication may be reproduced, copied, stored in a retrieval system or transmitted in any form or by any means electronic, mechanical, photocopying, recording or otherwise without prior written permission of the copyright owner.

Copyright © *ticktock* Entertainment Ltd 2005. First published in Great Britain in 2005 by *ticktock* Media Ltd, The Old Sawmill, 103 Goods Station Road, Tunbridge Wells, Kent, TN1 2DP.

Sub-topic 2 offers complete information about one aspect of the topic

Some suggested words to use in your project

The Glossary explains the meaning of any unusual or difficult words appearing on these two pages

Words to use in your project

arranged – planned
customs – traditions
childbirth – the process of giving birth to a baby
sanctuary – a safe place
settlement – a group of homes; village
spouse – a marriage partner

Glossary

alliances – unions by marriage, treaty or agreement
dowry – money or property paid by a woman's family to her new husband
morgengifu – money or property given to a woman by her new husband
turf – a slab of grass and earth
yarn – spun fibre for making cloth

See also: Religion 10–11; Towns 24–25; Law and Justice 28–29

Other pages in the book that relate to what you have read here are listed in this bar

have
childbirth

nen:

sweet,
; also

also
e

Viking women adorned their hair with combs.

19

The Case Study is a closer look at a famous person, artefact or building that relates to the topic

Captions clearly explain what is in the picture

Each photo or illustration is described and discussed in its accompanying text

CONTENTS

Saxons and Vikings

The departure of the Romans in about 408 CE left Britain undefended. Soon Saxons from Germany began raiding England, and by 600 CE, they began to settle there, along with the Angles from Denmark. By 789 CE, Danish and Norwegian Vikings began to raid England, Scotland and Ireland. From this time until the 11th century the Saxons and Vikings ruled Britain.

ALFRED THE GREAT

Saxon WARLORDS fought the Britons and by 800 CE had divided England into seven regions, each with its own king. Danish and Norwegian Vikings raided British coasts, until 865 CE, when they UNIFIED as one army. In 871 CE, the Danes attacked Wessex, and killed King Ethelred at the Battle of Ashdown. His brother Alfred became king. In 878 CE, Alfred defeated the Danes at the battle of Edington.

> ▶ **Source: The Life of King Alfred, by Asser, Bishop of Sherborne, 893 CE**
> The historian Asser, Bishop of Sherborne, wrote:
> *"Alfred attacked the whole PAGAN army, fighting ferociously … After fourteen days the pagans were brought to the extreme depths of despair by hunger, cold and fear, and they sought peace."*

Alfred NEGOTIATED the TREATY of Wedmore with Danish King Guthrum. By 886 CE, England was divided into the Viking-ruled Danelaw in the north, while Alfred ruled West MERCIA, Sussex and Kent.

Legend says that Alfred, preoccupied with the defence of his kingdom, burned some cakes, which he had been asked to look after.

KING CANUTE

Alfred died in 899 CE. In 1002, Alfred's successor, Ethelred 'The Unready', ordered the MASSACRE of the Danes in England, including the sister of the Viking king, Sweyn Forkbeard. Sweyn overthrew Ethelred in 1013 CE, but died shortly after. Sweyn's son, Canute, took the throne in 1016 CE. He successfully ruled an EMPIRE that covered England, Denmark, Norway and Sweden. According to the *Anglo-Saxon Chronicle* (9th–12th century), Canute sat on the beach and waited for the tide to come in to show that even he could not control everything.

King Canute waits for the tide to come in.

Words to use in your project

age – a period of time

blockade – a barricade

council – a gathering

dominion – a governed territory or country

hostility – a feeling of ill will

idolatry – worshipping an idol or idols

sovereign – a supreme monarch

Glossary

CE – Common Era

empire – many countries under one ruler

massacre – the deliberate killing of lots of people

Mercia – Saxon kingdom, now the Midlands area of England

negotiated – discussed to try to reach an agreement

pagan – a follower of a pre-Christian religion

treaty – a peace agreement

unified – to become one

warlords – regional leaders of a military force

See also: Viking Raids 6–7; Economy 14–15; Wars and Weapons 20–21; Language 22–23

CASE STUDY

Treaty of Wedmore

After Alfred and King Guthrum drew up the Treaty of Wedmore, Alfred insisted that Guthrum and his men should become Christian. Although the Vikings had their own religion, many accepted Christianity.

▸ **Source: The Anglo-Saxon Chronicle, written 9th–12th century**
This is an account of Guthrum's baptism:

"Then the army gave him hostages with many oaths, that they would go out of his kingdom. They told him also, that their king would receive baptism."

Map of England at the time of the Treaty of Wedmore.

Viking Raids

Vikings originated in the Scandinavian countries of Denmark, Sweden and Norway. As their population grew, there was not enough land for everyone, so they carried out raids on neighbouring countries, including Britain. They targeted monasteries – stealing treasures and capturing slaves.

CAUSES OF RAIDS

After the Romans departed, the Saxons started invading and settling. The Saxons had not only to fight the native Britons but also fought amongst themselves to start their individual kingdoms. As a result, they had no unified defence to fend off an enemy like the Vikings. The Vikings would often sail their longships onto the beach for a surprise attack. The spread of Christianity in the British Isles meant that there were many large monasteries. Vikings attacked the monastery at Lindisfarne, killing many monks and destroying their work.

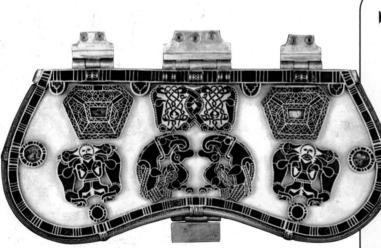

This purse lid was found in Sutton Hoo, Suffolk.

▶ **Source: The Anglo-Saxon Chronicle, written 9th–12th century**

A contemporary account describes the Viking attack at Lindisfarne:

"… there came for the first time three ships; and then the REEVE rode there and wanted to COMPEL them to go to the king's town, because he did not know what they were; and they killed him. Those were the first ships of the Danish men which sought out the land of the English race."

SHIPS

Although the Vikings are often remembered as raiders, they were also great explorers, traders, boatbuilders and NAVIGATORS. The wooden Viking longships were up to 30 metres long and could be sailed or rowed.

> ▶ *Source: Beowulf, author unknown, 8th–11th century*
>
> This epic poem describes the Vikings:
>
> *"They readied the ship on the waves under the cliffs and the warriors stood at the PROW as the water wound against the sand. The warriors bore into the ship's BOSOM bright weapons, fitted armour."*

Vikings raided with their mighty longships.

Words to use in your project

agrarian – agricultural
assault – to attack
epic – a long, exciting story
invasion – forced entrance
livelihood – a way of earning a living
sailing – travelling by water

Glossary

bosom – the centre or heart
compel – to force
navigators – people who plan a route of travel
prow – the front of a boat
reeve – a town official
slayed – killed

See also: Saxons and Vikings 4–5; Religion 10–11; Wars and Weapons 20–21; Towns 24–25

CASE STUDY

Raid on Lindisfarne

In 793 CE, Lindisfarne, off the coast of Northumberland, experienced the first Viking raid on Britain. The monks were unprepared for an attack, and may even have gone down to the shore to 'greet' the Vikings.

> ▶ *Source: The Anglo-Saxon Chronicle, written 9th–12th century*
>
> This account tells of the Viking attack:
>
> *"… wrecking, robbing, shattering and killing not only animals but also priests, monks and nuns … SLAYED everything alive, dug up the altars and took all the treasures of the holy church."*

Lindisfarne Abbey was the first to witness Viking raids in England.

Administration

Each Saxon region had its own rules. The DANELAW was governed by Viking rules for example, while the laws of the Kentish king Ethelbert (601–604 CE) were the first that were clearly not Roman. The southern-English king, Ine, introduced a new social order that included an ARISTOCRACY.

KINGSHIP

After Alfred's success at Edington he became recognized as the first king of England. Alfred allowed people to continue with farming and trade, while making sure that they were defended. He built a system of burghs (defensive market towns) across southern England, and people received plots of land in return for their willingness to fight. His army consisted of his thegns (royal followers) as well as the fyrd (professional warriors).

These 9th-century rings were probably symbols of royal office.

Thingvellir in Iceland has been the country's main meeting place since Viking times.

▶ **Source: The Anglo-Saxon Chronicle, written 9th–12th century**
In 890 CE, Alfred wrote:

"… A king's raw material and instruments of rule are a well-peopled land, and he must have men of prayer, men of war, and men of work."

VIKING TINGS

Early Viking culture allowed members of a TRIBE to seek VENGEANCE if one of their own people was killed or injured. The Viking Ting, or Thing, was introduced as a way to make local rules, and also to judge people accused of wrongdoings. Tings developed further into a way of solving DISPUTES, making laws, electing chiefs and taking political decisions.

> ▶ *Source: The Anglo-Saxon Chronicle, written 9th–12th century*
> The power of Tings are shown in this passage:
>
> *"Then King Canute proceeded; and, to be short in our tale, did not stop until he came to Trondheim, and landed at Nidaros. In Trondheim he called together a Thing for the eight districts, at which King Canute was chosen king of all Norway."*

Words to use in your project

concede – to yield, grant
dominate – to rule
execute – to carry out orders
mandate – an authoritative order or command
reorganize – to restructure
violator – a person failing to comply with the law

Glossary

aristocracy – the ruling class
Danelaw – an area of northern England ruled by the Vikings
disputes – disagreements
grievances – complaints
tribe – a group of linked people
vengeance – revenge

See also: Saxons and Vikings 4–5; Religion 10–11; Wars and Weapons 20–21; Towns 24–25

CASE STUDY

Manx Tynwald

Many modern parliaments are descended from the Viking Tings, including the Isle of Man's Tynwald. The High Court of Tynwald is the oldest continuous parliament in the world. Every year, around 5 July, members of both houses (the Legislative Council and the House of Keys) meet at the traditional open-air site of St John's at Tynwald Hill. On this day all people living on the Isle of Man can state their GRIEVANCES.

Regular Tings met at Tynwald Hill on the Isle of Man (a former Viking colony).

Religion

Christianity was introduced to Britain in Roman times, and a monastery was founded in 563 CE on Iona island, Scotland. The Saxons and Vikings worshipped many different gods and goddesses. In 597 CE, Pope Gregory sent the monk Augustine to Britain, to convert the Saxon leaders to Christianity.

MONASTIC REFORMS

After Augustine CONVERTED King Ethelbert, Christianity spread across southern England. Within 10 years, Christianity was the official religion of Kent, Sussex and London. Monasteries were built in Canterbury, Rochester and London, and Canterbury soon became the southern centre for Christianity. At about the same time, the work of Columba and his monks spread down from Scotland into northern England. A monastery was built on Lindisfarne island in 635 CE. The functions of Church and State became closely INTERWOVEN during this period.

▶ **Source: The Anglo-Saxon Chronicle, written 9th–12th century**
Here Bede describes the early days of Christianity:

"Churches were built in several places; the people joyfully flocked together to hear the Word; POSSESSIONS and lands were given of the King's BOUNTY to build monasteries."

Lindisfarne Castle on Lindisfarne Island.

VIKING GODS

Viking gods were split into two families called Vanir and Asar. They lived in a place called Asgard that was joined to Midgard (Earth) by the rainbow bridge Bifröst.

Odin was the most important Viking god. Another important god was Thor, the god of thunder. He was also the god of law and order, the champion of the people.

A Viking carving of the god Thor.

Words to use in your project

ceremony – a ritual
clergy – religious officials
confiscate – to seize (property)
deity – a god or goddess
faith – a belief in a divine power
purview – scope; extent or range of influence
sanction – approve

Glossary

bounty – generosity
converted – changed religious belief
interwoven – closely connected
possessions – things owned by somebody

See also: Administration 8–9; Food and Drink 16–17; Towns 24–25; Architecture and Art 26–27

CASE STUDY

Burials

Vikings believed that a person's spirit sailed to the next life. There, and on the journey, they would need certain possessions, which were buried with them. A Viking might be buried with a ship, or sent to sea in a burning longship.

▶ **Source: Ibn Fadlan, written after a voyage in 921 CE**
Arab chronicler Ibn Fadlan described a Viking burial:

"If the deceased is a poor man they make a little boat, which they lay him in and burn. If he is rich … then they pulled the ship up until it was on this wooden construction and set the ship on fire, so that the dead man and the ship are shortly burned to ashes."

Dead Viking warriors were often burned on their longships at sea.

Society

In Saxon England there were three broad classes of people: rulers, free people and slaves. Viking society was also divided into three similar areas. During Saxon times market towns, or burghs, started to grow, although farming remained the main part of the economy.

RICH AND POOR

The most important Saxons were the kings, and their princes (æelings). A ruling noble called an eolderman kept law and justice. He would summon the fyrd (professional warriors) and lead them in battle. There were many types of thegn (the main warriors of the fyrd) and higher thegns could become eoldermen. Ceorls were freemen, farmers and people who owned small areas of land. Slaves, or bondsmen, could own property and earn money in their own time.

> ▶ **Source: The Laws of Alfred, Guthrum and Edward the Elder, c. 10th century**
> Slaves tended to be looked after, as this extract tells:
>
> *"If a lord has his theow [slave] to work on a festival day let him pay LAHSIT within the Danish law, and WITE among the English."*

This 10th-century Viking arm ring would have been worn by a rich person to display his or her STATUS.

FARMERS AND TRADERS

Vikings and Saxons farmed the land and lived off the food they grew and animals they reared.

> **▶ Source: Ælfric's Colloquy, written about 1000 CE**
> Working on the farms was very hard:
>
> *"Ploughman: Oh my lord, I work very hard: I go out at dawn, driving the cattle to the field, and I YOKE them to the plough … I must plough one whole field a day, or more … it is a great labour for I am not free."*

Vikings had well-established trade routes with eastern European and Middle Eastern countries. Market towns (bugrhs) were places where farmers, craftsmen and merchants could trade. There were coins in Saxon and Viking times, but the BARTER system was often used at markets.

Most Vikings were full-time farmers and only part-time warriors.

Words to use in your project

adversary – a rival
commerce – the act of buying and selling
hierarchy – a status ranking system
occupation – a job
pastoral – associated with country life
regulated – controlled
traders – people buying and selling

Glossary

barter – to trade by exchanging goods
compensation – something given to make up for a loss
lahsit – a fine
status – position
wite – a fine
yoke – to harness

See also: Viking Raids 6–7; Economy 14–15; Language 22–23; Sports and Pastimes 30–31

CASE STUDY

Weregild and revenge

Both Saxon and Viking society had a system known as weregild, or blood money. It was a way to make sure that people were not killed as revenge for some wrong that had been done. Weregild provided COMPENSATION for the families of soldiers killed in battle. An agreed price would be paid out for the death of a man. Revenge was seen as the only way to restore honour in Saxon and Viking life.

> **▶ Source: Viking proverb**
> The idea of Viking revenge is explained in this saying:
>
> *"A slave takes revenge at once, a fool never takes revenge."*

Public killings were also used for vengeance, as seen on this picture stone from Lärbro parish of Gotland, Sweden.

Economy

Most of the trade and wealth in early Saxon times was created through agriculture. Farmers sold stock at markets and towns developed as major trading centres. Although the barter system was widely used, trade also helped to establish the use of coins.

TRADING

Farmers and craftsmen traded their goods and wares at markets. Getting goods to and from the market towns could be dangerous and difficult. The building of burghs (market towns with strong defensive walls) made trade safer, and became the site of MINTS.

Traders preferred to take their goods to market by boat as it was cheaper and quicker than by road.

> ▶ **Source: The Laws of King Edward the Elder, 901–924 CE**
>
> Buying was carefully REGULATED, as can be seen in this 10th century law:
>
> *"And that no man buy out of port, but have the port-reeve's witness, or that of other unlying men whom one may believe. And if any one buy out of port then let him incur the king's OFERHYRNES..."*

OVERSEAS trade was common for the Vikings and the importance of the Viking trading town Jorvik (now York) grew.

COINS

The first real Saxon coins, sceattas, were made of silver from about 600 CE. The penny was introduced to southern England in about 764 CE and became the DOMINANT CURRENCY. Pennies showed an image of the Saxon king. Viking rulers also produced coins for their trade.

The Saxon kings needed more and more mints to pay for war against the Vikings.

> ▶ **Source: The Laws of King Athelstan, 924–939 CE**
> King Athelstan passed this law in 928 CE saying that there was to be only one currency in England:
>
> *"… that there be one money over all the king's DOMINION, and that no man mint except within port. And if the moneyer be guilty, let the hand be struck off that wrought the OFFENCE, and, be set up on the money-smithy … "*

Words to use in your project

coinage – different coins
craft – to make with skill
export – to send goods to other countries
import – to bring in goods from other countries
ownership – to have possession of

Glossary

currency – a system of money
dominant – main
dominion – an area controlled by a king or queen
mints – places where coins are made
oferhyrnes – a special fine to be paid to the king for disobedience
offence – the act of breaking a law
overseas – relating to a foreign country
regulated – controlled

See also: Administration 8–9; Food and Drink 16–17; Law and Justice 28–29

CASE STUDY

Slavery

A Viking slave was called a thrall (male) or an ambatt (female). Viking slaves were often people captured during raids. The trade in slaves with Eastern European and Middle Eastern countries brought a lot of money to the economy. Saxon slaves were called deow, and they had a number of rights, including that of buying their freedom.

> ▶ **Source: The Laws of King Alfred, 871–899 CE**
> The rights of slaves were detailed in *The Laws of King Alfred*:
>
> *"All slaves ought to have Christmas supplies and Easter supplies, an acre for the plough and a 'handful of the harvest', in addition to their necessary rights."*

A man dressed in the clothing of a Saxon slave.

Food and Drink

The STAPLE diet for people at this time included meat, fish, vegetables, bread, fruits and grains. Most food was cooked in a large pot hung over an open fire. Saxons and Vikings usually ate from a wooden bowl or plate using only a knife, spoon or eating stick. They drank water, beer and MEAD.

THE SAXON DIET

For food, Saxons grew crops, reared and hunted animals, and gathered wild fruit. If they could afford to, they would trade at the market for other items they needed. Everything they ate was made by themselves, so they ground the wheat they had grown into flour and made it into bread. They were dependant on SEASONAL food that was available according to the time of year, as many kinds of food could not be PRESERVED.

They flavoured foods with HERBS. Sugar was not available, so honey was used to sweeten foods, and most Saxons kept their own bees.

Both Vikings and Saxons were expert fishermen. A lot of their fishing was in rivers and streams, but they also fished out at sea. They ate herring, salmon, eel, pike, perch and shellfish.

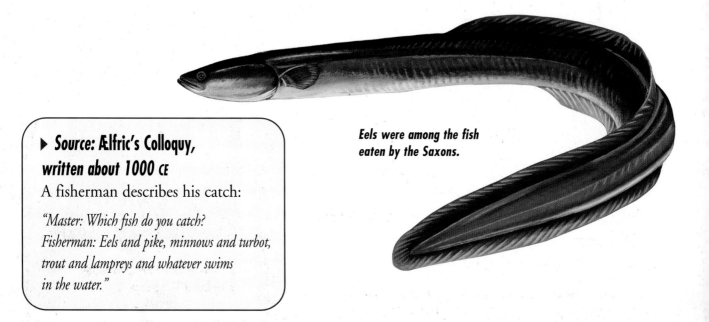

Eels were among the fish eaten by the Saxons.

> ▶ **Source: Ælfric's Colloquy, written about 1000 CE**
>
> A fisherman describes his catch:
>
> *"Master: Which fish do you catch?*
> *Fisherman: Eels and pike, minnows and turbot, trout and lampreys and whatever swims in the water."*

THE VIKING DIET

Meat, milk, eggs, wool and leather came from the cows, goats, pigs, sheep, chicken, ducks and geese that were kept. Meat was usually stewed. It was important to preserve meat and fish by smoking, drying or salting so that there was enough food to last through the winter.

Viking people hunted deer for meat.

> ▶ **Source: The Poetic Edda, a book of Viking poems and lore, c. 1250**
>
> Although both Vikings and Saxons made beer, heavy drinking was not encouraged, as explained in this traditional advice:
>
> *"Drink your mead, but in MODERATION, talk sense or be silent: No man is called discourteous who goes to bed at an early hour."*

Words to use in your project

cooperative – a group of people who help one another
farmland – land used for farming
flesh – meat
nutrition – food necessary for health and growth
recipe – the instructions for preparing a dish
taste – a sensation of flavour felt in the mouth

Glossary

herbs – plants used to flavour food or treat ailments
hide – an area of land
mead – a type of beer made from honey and barley
moderation – an average amount
preserved – prepared for storage
seasonal – according to the time of year
staple – main
theowman – a slave

See also: Society 12–13; Economy 14–15; Architecture and Art 26–27; Sports and Pastimes 30–31

CASE STUDY

Feasting

Feasts were held to celebrate holy days and special events, including weddings. Often guests were not allowed to leave the table until all the food was eaten. It was not unusual for a feast to last several days. Everyone, not just the aristocracy, enjoyed feasts. Slaves were allowed to join in some of the feasting.

> ▶ **Source: The Laws of Alfred, Guthrum and Edward the Elder, c. 10th century**
>
> Feasting was regulated by laws:
>
> *"If a freeman break a lawful feast, let him pay wite or lahslit. If a THEOWMAN do so, let him suffer in his HIDE or hide-gild."*

A 11th-century carving showing a typical Viking banquet.

Family and Marriage

Vikings lived in large family groups together in the same house. Saxon families built their homes close together. During the day the men, women and children spent most of their time on basic needs like growing and cooking food, making YARN and doing various crafts.

MARRIAGE

Saxon and Viking marriages were more about forming ALLIANCES than falling in love. Often families would arrange a marriage. The MORGENGIFU (literally, 'morning gift'), money and DOWRY that the two parties would bring to the marriage were settled before the wedding. After marriage, money and property belonged jointly to husband and wife.

Marriage in Viking society was a family affair. The extended family looked after the women and children should a husband be killed.

▶ **Source: The Laws of King Alfred, 871–899 CE**

Oaths and marriage vows were taken seriously, as this law of King Alfred shows:

"… it is most needful that every man warily keep his oath and his wed … if he pledge himself to that which it is lawful to fulfil, and in that belie himself … let him there suffer whatever the bishop may prescribe to him …"

DAILY LIFE

Vikings built wooden longhouses with a TURF roof. A house was usually just one room where the whole family ate and slept. It was dark and smoky inside as there were no windows or chimney, just a hole in the roof.

Viking longhouses were rectangular with just one room, similar to this cottage in the Shetland Islands.

▶ Source: Hávamál, a book of poems and advice, c. 950 CE

Most Vikings attached great importance to their home, as this quote shows:

"A small hut of one's own is better,
A man is his master at home:
A couple of goats and a corded roof
Still are better than begging."

Words to use in your project

arranged – planned
childbirth – the process of giving birth to a baby
customs – traditions
sanctuary – a safe place
settlement – a group of homes; village
spouse – a marriage partner

Glossary

alliances – unions by marriage, treaty or agreement
dowry – money or property paid by a woman's family to her new husband
morgengifu – money or property given to a woman by her new husband
turf – a slab of grass and earth
yarn – spun fibre for making cloth

See also: Religion 10–11; Towns 24–25; Law and Justice 28–29

CASE STUDY

A woman's role

The role of women was to run the house. Some women would have slaves or servants to help. Women were at great risk during childbirth as pregnancy was not fully understood.

▶ Source: Bald's Leechbook, c. 900 CE

This is an example of advice given to pregnant women:

"… ought to be fully warned against eating anything too salt or too sweet, and against drinking strong alcohol: also against pork and fatty foods; also against drinking to the point of drunkenness, also against travelling; also against too much riding on horseback lest the child is born before the right time."

Viking women adorned their hair with combs.

Wars and Weapons

The reputation of a ruler, and the territory he held, depended on his ability to win battles. Each ruler had his own band of warriors, who were fighting men from the area or professional MERCENARIES.

MILITARY ORGANIZATION

Each Saxon ruler had a fyrd, or small, loyal fighting force. Viking chiefs had similar bands of WARRIORS, called hird. The number of freemen (THEGNS or CEORLS) called upon to fight depended on the size of the area. A ROTA ensured that there were enough people left to keep producing food.

The Bayeux Tapestry (1050–1097) shows the Anglo-Saxon military during the Battle of Hastings.

> ▶ **Source: The Anglo-Saxon Chronicle, written 9th–12th century**
> From the early 9th century, the fyrd was regulated, as this account tells us:
>
> *"The king divided his army into two, so that always half of its men were at home, half on service, apart from the men who guarded the boroughs."*

WEAPONS AND ARMOUR

All men were expected to be armed, and the most common weapon was the spear. The most prized weapon was the sword, often handed down from father to son.

Heavy axes made better weapons for attack than defence.

> ▶ *Source: Beowulf, author unknown, 8th–11th century*
> The importance of a warrior's sword is related in Beowulf:
>
> *"Beowulf … then spoke some brave words before he got in bed, I don't claim myself any lower in strength or brave deeds than Grendel. Therefore, I will not kill him with a sword, though I easily might."*

Soldiers also carried heavy axes, helmets and strong shields. Soldiers overlapped their shields to produce a defensive wall.

Words to use in your project

allegiance – loyalty
bodyguards – armed troops that protect an important person
chivalry – valour
conquer – to overcome and gain control
courage – bravery
infantry – soldiers marching or fighting on foot

Glossary

ceorls – ordinary freemen
mercenaries – paid soldiers
Normandy – an area of northern France
rota – a system of regular change
thegns – fighting men
warriors – experienced soldiers
Witan – the Saxon ruling council

See also: Viking Raids 6–7; Administration 8–9; Society 12–13; Law and Justice 28–29

CASE STUDY

The Battle of Hastings

Edward the Confessor died in 1065, and the WITAN named Harold, Edward's brother-in-law, became king. Harald Hardrada of Norway saw his chance and landed an army in Yorkshire in September 1066. But Harold had a new enemy to face: Duke William of NORMANDY, who landed his men in southern England, claiming that Edward the Confessor had promised him the English throne. Harold returned south with his exhausted army and met William at the Battle of Hastings on 14 October. The Normans, with their superior archers and cavalry, won. Harold was killed.

This wall hanging is of the Battle of Hastings.

Language

No single language was spoken in Saxon and Viking Britain. Old English is the general name for the various GERMANIC dialects spoken by the Saxons, combined with Celtic. The Vikings spoke many DIALECTS of Old Norse, which also influenced the language spoken in Britain.

Widsith, one of the earliest English poems, was written in the 7th century.

OLD ENGLISH

Old English and Old Norse had many words in common. For example, the Old English word for a child was 'bearn', while in Old Norse it was 'barn'. The same word, 'bairn', is still used in Scotland and northern England. Old English can be hard to understand, but if you read a translation, many words become clearer.

The Old English alphabet is different from the modern English alphabet.

▶ Source: Ælfric's Colloquy, written about 1000 CE

[Teacher]: Hwæt hæfst ˛u weorkes?
[Pupil]: Ic eom geanwyrde monuc, ond sincge ælce dæg seofon tida mid gebro˛rum, ac ˛eahhwæ˛ere ic wolde betwenan leornian sprecan on leden gereorde.
[Teacher]: What is your work?
[Pupil]: I am a PROFESSED monk, and sing every day seven times with the BRETHREN, and I am busy, but nevertheless, between-times I learn to speak the LATIN language.

Many Saxon first names, including Edmund, Agnes and Edith, are still in use today. Job-related surnames including Baker, Weaver, Fisher, Fowler and Hunter, have also survived. A Viking's surname showed the name of a man's mother or father, so, Harald, son of Eric, would be Harald Eriksson.

ANGLO-SAXON POETRY

Old English poetry often told heroic tales of Viking history, or Christian stories of morals and beliefs. Many Old English poems, including *Beowulf*, *Widsith*, *Deor* and *The Wanderer*, tell of the past and compare it to the difficulties of present life.

> ▶ **Source: The Seafarer, an Anglo-Saxon poem, c. 970 CE**
>
> *The Seafarer* presents a BLEAK picture of a world that has lost its splendour:
>
> *"Now there are no captains or kings, or gold-givers as there once were when they did most glorious deeds … joys have departed; the weak remain to rule this world …"*

Words to use in your project

ancestor – a person from whom another is descended
mother tongue – a native language
mythology – stories and legends of a culture
nostalgia – affection for the past

Glossary

bleak – depressing
brethren – brotherhood
dialects – local languages or speech
Germanic – relating to Germany
Latin – the language that was used for religious ceremonies
oral – spoken
professed – claimed openly

See also: Wars and Weapons 20–21; Architecture and Art 26–27

CASE STUDY

Runes

Most Vikings and Saxons could not read or write, so they used the ORAL tradition of reciting stories. Symbols called runes were also used, with each rune having a separate meaning. The Vikings and Saxons considered runes to be magical.

> ▶ **Source: Hávamál, a book of poems and advice, c. 950 CE**
>
> *Hávamál* shows how a man used runes to raise a ghost:
>
> *"A twelfth [spell] I know: when I see aloft upon a tree*
> *A corpse swinging from a rope,*
> *Then I cut and paint runes*
> *So that the man walks*
> *And speaks with me."*

Runes are a key to understanding the lives and beliefs of ancient people.

Towns

The Saxons added to Roman towns and also built new ones for defensive purposes. Towns contained market places, workshops, MINTS, ADMINISTRATIVE centres and GARRISONS for soldiers. Vikings tended to live in the countryside, but they soon developed Jorvik (York) into a trading town.

LIFE IN TOWNS

Saxon towns developed because of the need for local markets and fairs, and centres for worship and justice. The name 'tun' was used for these new towns or places. Towns were also places of safety as many were surrounded by a defensive wall or fence. Alfred's plan for 33 BURGHS meant that most people were within 30 kilometres of a safe HAVEN.

▶ **Source: The Life of King Alfred, by Asser, Bishop of Sherborne, 893 CE**
The chronicler Asser describes Alfred's building work:

"...the towns and cities he restored, and others which he built where none had been before."

Towns were sometimes destroyed in war and had to be rebuilt, as with London in 886 CE:

"Alfred ... after the burning of the cities and the slaying of the people, honourably rebuilt the city of London, and made it again HABITABLE."

Viking settlements were groups of homes surrounded by a wooden fence.

LONDON AND YORK

Jorvik (York) grew to be the major town in the Danelaw and the centre for trade with Europe and further AFIELD. People came to trade goods and crafts, pottery, leather work and weaving. London had been a substantial Roman city. The River Thames made it easy to transport goods and it developed as a place for trade. London became the seat of kings and a focus for wars.

A reconstruction of Jorvik (York).

▶ **Source: The Life of King Alfred, by Asser, Bishop of Sherborne, 893 CE**
The Vikings attacked London several times:

"… with three hundred and fifty ships to the mouth of the river Thames, and sacked … the city of London, which lies on the north bank of the river Thames."

Words to use in your project

arson – the act of setting on fire maliciously
flourishing – prosperous
headquarters – an administrative centre
inhabitant – a citizen
issue – to circulate
network – a system
safeguard – to protect

Glossary

administrative – relating to an organization
afield – far away
burghs – defensive market towns
garrisons – places where soldiers are based
habitable – fit to live in
haven – a safe place
mints – places where coins are made

See also: Saxons and Vikings 4–5; Administration 8–9; Economy 14–15; Sports and Pastimes 30–31

CASE STUDY

Burghs

Planned by Alfred the Great, burghs were the first 'national' defence system. They were located mainly along the border with the Danelaw and could accomodate people during enemy raids. Malmesbury, in Wiltshire, is one of the oldest Saxon burghs.

▶ **Source: description of Malmesbury by the 16th-century historian John Leland**
"The toun of Malmesbyri stondith on the very toppe of a greate slaty rok, and ys wonderfully defended by nature."

Malmesbury Abbey in the Saxon burgh of Malmesbury.

Architecture and Art

Most Saxon homes were constructed from a wooden frame and walls of WATTLE and DAUB. Stone was used to build churches and monasteries. Vikings also used timber for building.

CHURCHES

Few wooden Saxon buildings in England have survived. However, there are examples of stone buildings like monasteries and churches.

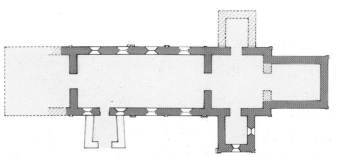

This plan shows the typical layout of a Saxon church.

Early Saxon churches had a simple layout, usually just a long rectangular shape that ran east to west. The inside of the church was plain except for a few carved stone panels.

▶ **Source: The Life of King Alfred, by Asser, Bishop of Sherborne, 893 CE**

King Alfred's chronicler, Asser, describes Saxon construction:

"Of the royal halls and chambers, wonderfully built of stone and of wood at his command? Of royal VILLS made of masonry removed from the old sites and most admirably rebuilt in more suitable places by the king's order."

St Mary's in Breamore, Hampshire, is a Saxon church from around 1000 CE.

SAXON HOMES

The homes of ordinary Saxon and Viking people were simple and small.

> ▶ *Source: Beowulf, author unknown, 8th–11th century*
>
> Wealthy Saxons had large houses, richly decorated with designs or pictures on the walls, as described by the writer of *Beowulf*:
>
> *"… And he resolved to build a hall, a large and noble feasting-hall of whose splendours men would always speak … Then I heard that tribes without number, were given orders to decorate the hall."*

A reconstructed Saxon settlement at West Stow, Suffolk.

Words to use in your project

dense – compact
design – an arrangement for artistic effect
habitation – a living place
masonry – stonework

Glossary

anchorite – a person living in a monastery
daub – sticky plaster
gilded – covered with a thin layer of precious metal
unalloyed – pure
vills – estates
wattle – woven twigs used for building

See also: Religion 10–11; Society 12–13; Economy 14–15; Towns 24–25; Family and Marriage 18–19

CASE STUDY

Art and craft

Viking crafts were usually practical, such as the elaborate brooches used by women to secure their dresses or intricate grave carvings. Creatures in linked patterns were common and also used in Christian Saxon art, as seen in the Lindisfarne Gospels. The Gospels are masterpieces of book production.

> ▶ *Source: The Anglo-Saxon Chronicle, written 9th–12th century*
>
> This is a description of the Lindisfarne Gospels being made:
>
> *"Æthelwald, Bishop of the Lindisfarne islanders, bound it on the outside and covered it, as he knew well how to do. And Billfrith, the ANCHORITE, wrought the ornaments on the outside and adorned it with gold and with gems and GILDED silver, UNALLOYED metal …"*

An illustrated page from the Lindisfarne Gospels.

Law and Justice

Saxon kings were responsible for maintaining law and order. There were no prisons, and people were often punished with a fine. For some crimes, a nose or a hand could be cut off. If a person hurt or killed someone, he had to pay money, known as weregild, to the victim's relatives.

TAKING OATH

The Saxon law was that an ACCUSED person was presumed innocent until proven guilty. The DEFENDANT would SWEAR an oath, and find others who would swear to his innocence.

Swearing an oath in court was taken seriously by the Vikings and Saxons.

> ▶ **Source: The Laws of Alfred, Guthrum and Edward the Elder, c. 10th century**
>
> Under the law of King Alfred, a defendant would swear with the words:
>
> *"By the Lord, I am guiltless, both in deed and COUNSEL, and of the charge of which [person's name] accuses me."*
>
> Those not considered honest enough to take an oath could put forward witnesses, who would swear:
>
> *"In the name of Almighty God ... I saw with my eyes and heard with ears that which I pronounce with him."*

A person who was guilty would find it difficult to persuade others to support him. Courts were small and everyone knew one another.

TRIAL BY ORDEAL

Trial by ORDEAL was used only if the accused could not find others to support him. For ordeal by water, the accused was thrown into a river or pond. If he floated, he was judged guilty, and if he sank, he was innocent. Ordeal by fire would involve being burned by hot iron bars. If the wound festered, the man was guilty.

> ▶ **Source: The Laws of King Athelstan, 924–939 CE**
>
> This is an extract explaining one of the rules relating to trial by ordeal:
>
> *"And concerning the ordeal we enjoin by command of God, and of the archbishop, and of all the bishops: that no man come within the church after the fire is BORNE in with which the ordeal shall be heated, except the MASS-PRIEST, and him who shall go thereto..."*

Words to use in your project

admission – a confession
district – an area
judiciary – a group of judges
proof – evidence that establishes the truth
statute – a law
testimony – a written or spoken statement

Glossary

accused – brought formal charges against someone
borne – carried
counsel – advice
defendant – a person accused in a court of law
mass-priest – the priest who says mass in church
ordeal – a method of trial in which the accused is exposed to physical danger
swear – to make a declaration by an appeal to something sacred

See also: Religion 10–11; Society 12–13; Family and Marriage 18–19

CASE STUDY

Laws in the hundreds

As Saxon England became unified, laws governing the whole land were passed. The king and the witan (senior council) considered issues and agreed laws. Eoldermen and thegns made sure they were applied in their area.

> ▶ **Source: The Laws of King Æthelberht, 560–616 CE**
>
> Punishments (usually fines) were set out, like these from 6th-century Kent:
>
> *"If a shoulder be lamed, let bot [payment] be made with thirty shillings. If an ear be struck off, let bot be made with twelve shillings. Let him who breaks the chin-bone pay for it with twenty shillings."*

Fines were imposed for many crimes in Saxon England.

Sports and Pastimes

Most of the games played challenged either the physical or mental strengths of the participants. Music, poetry, storytelling and solving riddles were also popular, and took place at fairs and market gatherings.

Musical instruments of Viking times included whistles made of bone and wooden PAN PIPES.

GAMES PLAYED

Wrestling and weightlifting were popular, although very rough – contestants often ended up with broken bones. Ball games rather like hockey, hurling or shinty were played. Juggling was popular both as a test of skill and for entertainment. Five stones was a game like the modern jacks, and nine men's morris was similar to draughts. Other sports included BEAR-BAITING.

Board games were very popular with Vikings.

> ▶ **Source: Sverris saga, c. 1200 CE**
> This extract involves performing dogs:
>
> *"Two players … who made small dogs jump over high poles in front of high born men, and the more high born they were the higher they jumped."*

Board games were popular during the Saxon and Viking period. Early chess pieces found on the Scottish Isle of Lewis are believed to be of 10th-century Viking origin.

MUSIC AND STORYTELLING

A favourite PASTIME was music and storytelling. Vikings enjoyed tales of their gods and other heroic events.

> ▶ **Source: Widsith, an Anglo-Saxon poem, c. 7th century**
>
> A scop (poet and storyteller) would perform for kings and rich people, as is in the 7th-century poem *Widsith*:
>
> *"When Scilling [Widsith's harp] and I, with a clear voice, raised the song before our royal lord, loud with the harp I sounded the melody."*

Dancing and music were enjoyed and there were professional musicians, called gleemen who played at feasts and other special occasions. People played a range of instruments, including harps, LYRES, and whistles.

Words to use in your project

competition – sporting activity
oral – spoken
participate – take part
puzzle – a game to test knowledge
recreation – entertainment
restriction – limit
sprint – run at full speed

Glossary

bear-baiting – a sport in which a bear is attacked by many dogs
lyres – small harp-like instruments
pan pipes – a musical instrument played by blowing across a row of pipes
pastime – a way of spending spare time
smiths – people who make or repair metal objects

See also: Food and Drink 16–17; Family and Marriage 18–19

CASE STUDY

Riddle-me-ree

Many Saxon riddles had double meanings, and were often in rhyme.

> ▶ **Source: Exeter Book, 1070 CE**
>
> This was a popular Saxon riddle:
>
> *"I'm by nature solitary, scarred by spear and wounded by sword, weary of battle. I frequently see the face of war, and fight hateful enemies; yet I hold no hope of help being brought to me in the battle, before I'm eventually done to death. In the stronghold of the city sharp-edged swords, skillfully forged in the flame by SMITHS bite deeply into me. I can but await a more fearsome encounter; it is not for me to discover in the city any of those doctors who heal grievous wounds with roots and herbs. The scars from sword wounds gape wider and wider death blows are dealt me by day and by night."*

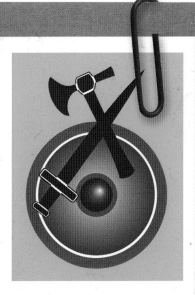

The answer to the riddle is a shield.

Index

Saxon & Viking Timeline

793 CE

Vikings attack the monastery at Lindisfarne (Holy Island).

865 CE

Vikings fight as one large army of Danes.

871 CE

King Ethelred killed at the Battle of Ashdown. Alfred becomes king.

878 CE

Alfred defeats the Danes at the Battle of Edington.

886 CE

England divided into the Viking-ruled Danelaw in the north, while Alfred rules the south.

893 CE

Asser, the Bishop of Sherborne, writes The Life of King Alfred.

899 CE

Ethelred 'The Unready' becomes king.

1013 CE

Sweyn Forkbeard overthrows Ethelred, but dies the following year.

1016 CE

Canute crowned king, and rules over a large, prosperous empire.

1042 CE

Edward the Confessor becomes king.

1065 CE

Edward dies and Harold is named king.

October 1066 CE

Harold defeated at the Battle of Hastings. William, Duke of Normandy, becomes king.

PICTURE CREDITS: Ancient Art Library: 4–5 all, 8–9 all, 10b, 10–11c, 21 all, 22–23 all, 24–25 all, 28b, 31c. **Corbis:** 13 all, 14–15 all, 28r, 28–29t. **Hemis.fr/Superstock:** OFC main. **iStock:** 1 and throughout, OBCc. **Mary Evans:** 6–7 all, 12b, 26t, 27 all, 18b, 19c, 20b. **Jorvik Viking Centre:** 30–31c. **Look and Learn/Bridgeman Art Library:** OFCt and OFCb. **Shutterstock:** OBCb.